HEALTHY MENTAL

A healthy mind completes a person.
Always strive for completeness

M. Minott

Monika Minott

authorHOUSE®

AuthorHouse™ UK
1663 Liberty Drive
Bloomington, IN 47403 USA
www.authorhouse.co.uk
Phone: 0800.197.4150

Published by AuthorHouse 11/16/2016

ISBN: 978-1-5246-6363-6 (sc)
ISBN: 978-1-5246-6362-9 (hc)
ISBN: 978-1-5246-6364-3 (e)

Introduction

From someone who was nearly pushed over the edge, to now balancing a healthy mental lifestyle, how I achieved it? I fought back. Why? Because I am worth it.

In this fast paced world of relentless pressures, deadlines, stress, work, families, illnesses, bills and loss. It is becoming increasingly difficult to keep everything afloat and to live balanced lives. Want to talk about a tight rope and balancing that, yes! Life can seem like a circus, a merry go round and that's putting it mildly. From my experience, life is no longer simple, quiet and nice; it's hectic, mad and challenging on a daily basis.

What I want to achieve in this little book of healthy mental is to expose some of the signs of mental illnesses, how it affects us, how to attack bad feelings and thoughts when they come upon you and simply how to change not only the negative perception you may have about someone with a mental illness but how you can challenge and maintain your own mental state of mind in a positive and healthy way.

I want to show you ways to help you cope with the stress and strains of life when they come upon you, and highlight the different support groups available at the clip of a button. I want you to be aware that you are not totally helpless in your situation that there are countless ways to help yourself by using what you have ie your gifts and skills, your own resources to not only protect your mind but to be able to use it as an outlet when life gets too difficult for you. I would always advise someone to seek professional help and advice first before embarking on anything else. I also want to highlight to families the ways they can support a loved one with a mental illness and the support that is out there for them as well, as all too often family members and carer's are left without support. I hope this book will help you to live a healthier mental lifestyle and maybe prevent you from going into the mental health system.

Contents

*Be a man of understanding and understand that everyone
does not understand the things you do.*

Author unknown

Chapter 1

What is mental illness?

It is a distorted way of thinking due to malfunction of the brain, a disease of the brain. It can range from mild to severe. Its results are disturbances in thought and or behaviour and this can affect the way a person copes and lives in their everyday life. There are over 200 forms of mental health diagnosis, ranging from dementia to depression and general symptoms also vary between different types and may include mood changes, personality changes and withdrawal symptoms.

Although the exact cause of mental illness is unknown, research has shown that a combination of genetic, psychological and environmental factors plays a role. It is not down to a person being weak and careless with their life. It is important to know that in-order for a person to recover it is down to a number of interventions working together for best and long lasting results.

My personal view of mental illness is that its:

A state of mind that is not in line with the rest of the body, i.e your mind and body should be working together in a healthy way, in unison, as you are one person. When one is out of line with the other, having conflicting messages, ideas, thoughts and or behaviours, this will and can only delude you and throw everything out of sync.

It is not always easy or possible to have this beautiful unison at all times, but that is the ideal unison when mind and body are working nicely together, In fact, many times you will not have the union of both working together. There will be times when they are both out of balance due to situations, experiences, problems and simply how you are feeling at the time. But when you are conscious of this fact you will find that balance is quickly regained and at least try to maintain it during your lifetime. Maintenance is the key here.

Maintenance

There will be times when your mind is telling you or prompting you to do something that is good for you, then your whole being needs to step in line with your mind and work for the betterment of the whole body, a wholesome you. An example is when a person wants to lose weight, it first starts in the mind, then the rest of the body follows or should follow by actions to work towards that achievement or goal of losing weight. After the thought, discipline, determination, motivation, encouragement, a goal and well thought out plan, a realistic plan. I know that does not always work, but that's how it should work.

A mental illness is not down to the colour of your skin; it's not specific to profession, race/ethnic group or religion. Most people either knows, knows about or is related to someone who suffers from a mental condition. Mental health can affect anyone at any time for any reason, sometimes for reasons that may seem very simple to others. Someone is not just tipped over the edge over night, it is normally something that has been brewing for some time and then as we have all heard the term, 'the straw that broke the camel's back' yes! That one little thing that tips someone over the edge, (but in fact that person was moving towards the edge for some time) they just didn't realize it, sometimes from childhood. Have you also heard there is a thin line between sanity and insanity? well this is it. Some of us are literally living our lives on that thin line, due to daily pressures of life, which in the end overcomes us, not by choice I might add but more of a tipping of the balance in the wrong direction.

At times it could be that one tragedy, that a person will experience in their life and that experience can be so traumatic it tips a person into thinking and behaving in a wrong way and that person may never totally recover that balance that is needed for healthy living. This is when counselling, or medical professional advice or support is needed or some kind of intervention as it may sometimes help to regain the balance needed for healthy living mentally, hence a healthier life. We all go through things that get us down, low and depressed but it is really how you handle your struggles that will make a difference to any outcome.

An example of a point in my life when I felt the pressure of life closing in on me was when my son had just started primary school. We faced some challenges quite early on. There was always something for the teachers to report about his behaviour

3

i.e He didn't listen today, he didn't follow the rules yesterday, he is displaying inappropriate behaviour, he did this and he did that. It was endless and there was a constant trickle of complaints throughout the years, which frequently left me feeling low and I was at a point very worried about him. The teachers turned minor issues into insurmountable difficulties. I was low and sometimes felt depressed, but we never gave up on our son, even though it was hard for me. I did not feel I was supported enough but I kept pressing on with the issues that faced me head on.

I attended meetings upon meetings to discuss issues and to try to find solutions, and we did, things got much better, his behaviour improved. My son was appointed a black male mentor in year 4 which he responded to tremendously, well to the mentor. Not that I thought other teachers did not impact on him but his mentor seemed to have had a more positive affect with him. When he reached year five things started to settle even more, he became more mature and started to take more responsibility for his actions and generally seemed happier and grew in confidence and self-belief. I was happier too, I believe a large part of my son's challenges was because he felt he did not fit into the norm but believed he was the exception to every rule in the classroom.

I'm not saying I had an angel for a son but my son was not a naughty child either, he was a child that did not conform as quickly as the other kids in the classroom. Academically he is very bright and I strongly believe that he was not challenged academically, the consequence of which led to him displaying behaviours, which the teachers found difficult to cope with at first and branded him a naughty child.

There was a point where they were insinuating that there was something mentally wrong with him. I know that the teachers have it hard with having 30 something children in a classroom, deadlines to meet, books to mark and they definitely needed some discipline and order in the classroom to carry out their duties. With that being said it did not stop me having sleepless nights and days full of worry. Looking back now I see that they were only minor incidents that needed to be ironed out. I worked closely with the teachers and we kept each other informed and supported at all times. By the time he left primary school his behaviour was very much an acceptable one, but hay boys will definitely be boys. Our son is now in secondary school and is doing just fine and I thank God for that. All our efforts have not gone wasted. I'm glad I did not give up on him and that I challenged and pressed on or things could have been very different.

I shared this story because many parents can relate to this and I know deep down every parent just want the best for their children. I know also that many times it is our children that put pressure on us. We may not own up to it but this is true. We worry when they are young then we worry when they are older. We need to give ourselves a little slack. It takes a nation to grow a child, so use any and every resource available to you to ease the pressure of growing up your children in today's society. When my husband and I were looking at the issues our son was going through, we thought if we got him involved in activities outside of school and home, it would keep him stimulated and focused. Something, anything that would give him a sense of pride, something he could work towards. We tried a few activities such football and tae-quando but these did not really work for him. It was suggested by my sister, to try music, singing and playing an instrument, and this worked, he not only shows great skill in playing the piano but he also has a real interest in it and goals to work towards. Playing the piano has also helped him in school as he plays in assemblies and has helped in giving him the focus and challenge he needed to settle in his new environment.

Daily Pressures

These kind/types of daily pressures can cause us to be depressed. You may not look at depression as a mental health condition but if left untreated can become dangerous to our mental health and possibly, eventually needing long-term medication. I'm not saying that our children cause us to have mental ill health but the worry of our children can cause not only mental but physical conditions. We need to bear that in mind. We need to be aware of the daily pressures that we face and deal with and how it affects us. We need to think of many ways to get the help and support we need with our problems and look for solutions, rather than suffering on our own. There will be many people going through the same kind of problem I had to go through. Many times when we talk about our problems, there is someone who can shed some light on our situation and offer us the advice we need. Don't think for one minute you have to go it alone.

Chapter 2

Causes of Mental Illnesses

Causes can range from physical to emotional and bring about confused thinking and behaviours. An example is when an elderly person who already has a condition such as dementia and when coupled with a urinary tract infection can cause confusion and or delirium. This is one out of many examples.
Reference: www.alzheimers.org.uk.

In my opinion, anything and everything can be a trigger to a mental condition. *A quote by Randy Pausch said, it's not the cards you are dealt with in life, it's how you play them that matters. www.goodreads.com*

This will and can make all the difference in the outcome of your circumstances. It is imperative then that we deal with everyday problems in a positive way in order to get the results we desire that will bring about best outcomes for our mental, physical, spiritual and emotional wellbeing. I know! Easier said than done.

When faced with problems all I want to do is scream, shout and throw things, but I also know that that does not get anyone anywhere least of all me. I strongly believe that it is necessary to have some kind of positive outlet to help bring us through the problems or issues in our lives. Then look at resolutions rather than suffering it alone.

When problems, pressures and issues of life are kept bottled within us, it not only affects our mental health, it will and can cause physical deterioration. Ever noticed that when some people are faced with issues of mental illnesses they also have physical problems too, which is sometimes seen later. Some people are known to have an increased risk of heart disease, respiratory disease, certain types of cancer and weight gain. (2nd Sept 2016) *www.mentalhealth.org.* This is not the case with everyone, some people look absolutely fine, but underneath they are crying out for help. This may seem like a sweeping statement but usually that is the case with a lot of people suffering from a mental illness. When your mental health is not healthy it sometimes has a bearing on how you present yourself to the world, it has a bearing on how you eat, sleep, feel, your general lifestyle and ultimately the outcome of how you look and interact with the world.

We all know that some of the medications have negative side effects. Don't get me wrong, medications are an important factor and has been a great help to many people suffering from a mental illnesses and without them, some of these people would not be able to cope or function on a daily basis. However the side effects of some of the medications can have negative consequences and cause many people to not want to take them. Many people end up having to be sectioned because they have not taken their medications. Many times, sufferers take their medications and do feel better then they stop again, it becomes a cycle over and over again. They feel in their minds that they are better and that they don't need to continue taking their medications. This is an illusion because as they stop their lives tend to deteriorate slowly and before they know it they are back to square one, Because some medications are known to cause weight gain, hallucinations, paranoia and many more. My view is that medications should be a last resort. I am just touching the surface here literally as **I am no expert**. So let's get back to the causes shall we. To list just a few, the causes of mental health problems can be:

1 **Hereditary**, it has been proven by scientists that certain genes can be passed on through family, making you pre-disposed to developing a mental illness. If you then are already prone to mental illness, coupled with a bad environment, experience and or trauma ect. Can and will trigger the onset of the disease

2 **Abuse** (Emotional, Physical, psychological and sexual) Abuse can or will take its toll on your life sooner or later. Even though you may have had some kind of intervention, such as therapy. The trauma never leaves you, but you learn to live with the scars as best you can. You cannot wipe out memories from your brain. They cannot be totally erased but they can be replaced with positive memories and thoughts. We all have bad experiences in our lives but we have some control over how we choose to deal with them. Intervention such as counselling have been proven to have positive effects when you are able to talk about the problems, at best and mostly when there is some stability

in your life already and you feel comfortable talking about your issues, this is where counselling is very effective. Many people are then able to live a healthy happy life.

3 **Loss,** the loss of a loved one, of a limb ect. Loss of anything can cause mental health illness, it does not matter what that loss is. Many people who lose a pet, to them it's like losing a loved one. It is argued that the effects of loss are all the same, no matter what that loss is. It just has varying degrees of potency upon one's life. Loss can cause loneliness, which could then lead to the onset of another type of illness that you may have to deal with. We cope with loss all the time, loss of jobs and the stress it puts on a family.

4 **Trauma** (accident/incident) Trauma of any type has lasting effects on a person's mind and can follow them through their entire life. We are all different and we all cope in different ways to the same situation. You have to find your inner strength, your way of coping. As I said before it's not the cards you are dealt it's how you play them. Life has handed you a deck of cards, know the game, play them well and use your mind, your skills and your intuition. Play the best game of life you can. We only have one life make the most of it.

5 **Physical illnesses,** the effects of physical illness can not only cause depression but can also bring a life of uncertainty to the person suffering. A person may feel like their life is stagnant because there is very little they can do to change their circumstances because of the pain they may be feeling. So their future may look bleak and hopeless. Physical illnesses can not

only cripple you physically but also cripple you mentally and your outlook on life can seem desolate. When there is unmanaged physical pain, emotional pain is never far away and when it is not managed this can and will only make the case worse for the person suffering. It is our responsibility to manage our illnesses as best we can, Physical and mental pain. Find out about your illness, do your research and look at ways that you can help yourself and allow the doctors to do their bit.

6 **Stress** (pressures of life, pressures of work, family pressures) pressure of any kind that is continuous can be very negative to the body. This puts the body under strain that sometimes cannot be physically seen. The body needs to be restored, replenished and refilled on a daily basis and I mean, the mind and your physical body. Resting the body is not enough. Your mind needs to be able to focus on positive things. If this restoration decreases continuously, problems can appear and begin to manifest into your everyday life. So it is important to rest and look at rest as an inclusive of mind body and soul.

These are the main causes that we can all relate too as we would may have experienced one of these challenges ourselves, or know someone going through, or has gone through, have one of these examples. Mental health does not single out one person or groups of people but it can affect us all at any time so guard your precious mind.

You may find that in some types of professions, some people can be more prone to developing a mental health illness. For example, soldiers at war, we have all seen and heard of men and women who have gone to war who later experience war type mental illnesses, Such as Post-traumatic stress syndrome. Especially when left untreated. Veterans who fought for our cause, returns home wounded not only physically but mentally and emotionally. Losing friends along the way and witnessing the terrible atrocities of war must be heart breaking; yet they come home and are expected to resume a normal life with their families and friends, which is almost an impossibility. Are they are expected to just pick up from where they left off, without any kind of continuous support or intervention? I am aware that there is support out there for men and women in the army but is it enough?

This is not only reduced to soldiers at war but to those actually in warzone countries. They would have also seen the negative effects of war on their lives. Sadly, many men, women and children do not get the support they need during and post war period even after seeking asylum leaving or if the war has stopped. They suffer the effects of war for the rest of their lives with mental, emotional and physical ill health. This also demonstrates how important it is to have counselling or some intervention early on, not only in the career of soldiers but for those in war countries to minimize the effects of their experiences and the negative impact on their lives. Rehabilitation for soldiers or anyone going through a mental illness has to be an on-going and consistent process to try to undo some of the damage that has been caused.

Chapter 3

Some of the most common types of mental illness

There is a whole host of different types of mental illnesses. I will list some of the most common types that we may all be familiar with including symptoms. As mentioned earlier in the book, there are over 200 different types.

1 **Anxiety disorders**, symptoms incl; a sense of dread, feeling constantly on edge, difficulty concentrating, restlessness irritability, feeling sick, dizziness and trembling or shaking (reference)

2 **Mood disorders**, symptoms incl; depression and bipolar, well known as manic-depressive, prolonged sadness, unexplained bouts of crying, feelings of guilt, withdrawal, suicidal thoughts, anger and worry.

3 **Psychotic disorders**, symptoms incl; Delusions, paranoia, visual and auditory hallucinations and finding it hard to make decisions. These may vary from one person to another

4 **Eating disorders**, such as bulimia, anorexia nervosa, binge eating disorder, over eating disorders and pica. Symptoms may

vary depending on the type of disorder. Skipping meals, excessive need to eat healthy foods only, eating alone and not with family, obsession about weight control, eating large amounts of junk foods such as sweets, cakes, of high calories/fat foods and excessive exercise.

5 **Impulse control and addiction disorders**; symptoms may include a failure to resist a temptation or temptations. An urge or impulse that may harm self and or others. Concerns with or problems with self-control. The five behavioural stages are growing tension, pleasure on acting, and relief from the urge and possible guilt. Behaviours such as compulsive sexual drive and shopping can also be seen in this disorder.

6 **Personality disorders**, such as paranoid personality disorder, schizoid personality disorder and antisocial personality disorder all come under the same umbrella. Symptoms may include distrust, having a suspicious mind, thoughts of others lying about them, inability to enjoy life, little interest in forming relationships, a belief in secret messages and special powers, lack of concern, cannot control anger very well and lack of guilt. These are just a few examples of the many different types of personality disorders.

7 **Obsessive-compulsive disorders**, symptoms may include having an obsession with lists and trying to put things in order, when one is unable to delegate tasks to others, obsession with saving money and being a workaholic.

8 **Post-traumatic stress disorders**, in most cases the symptoms start about 4-5 weeks after the trauma but will vary from person to person. Symptoms may include, flashbacks, nightmares, pain, sweating, and trembling, sleeping problems and angry outbursts. There are a number of different types of post-traumatic stress disorder and symptoms can range from mild to severe.

9 **Stress response syndrome**; symptoms may include the sufferer becoming emotionally detached, de-realization, depersonalization, re-experiencing a trauma or event by thoughts, dreams and or flashbacks, avoidance of an event that may remind them of the trauma.

10 **Dissociative disorder**; symptoms may include memory loss with people, events and experiences. Depression, suicidal thoughts or attempts, a thinking that people is unreal or distorted. A distorted sense of identity, general problems at work, in relationships and other important areas in life.

11 **Sexual and gender disorders**; symptoms may include a very strong desire to be the opposite sex, cross-dressing, wanting to participate in activities or games of which would be designed for the opposite sex. When a person actually states that they want to be of the opposite sex. Feeling uncomfortable with the gender role of sexual encounters or during sex.

12 **Somatic symptom disorder**; symptoms may include pain; shortness of breath and weakness but is unrelated to any known medical condition or cause. The symptoms come with excessive thoughts or actions of what the person is feeling. The sufferer

will interpret any normal sensation of the body as a symptom of a serious illness.

13 **Tic disorder; symptoms,** every person experiences tics differently, the most noticeable is Tourette's syndrome where both physical and verbal tics occur in the same person. A sufferer may raise their eyebrows, shrug their shoulders and flare nostrils, click their tongue or make a certain vocal sounds. This differs from person to person.

14 **Bipolar disorder**; symptoms may include insomnia, rapid speech, racing ideas, reckless behaviour, intense ideas and energy and bizarre behaviour.

15 **Body dysmorphic disorder**; symptoms include constantly looking at yourself in the mirror and looking for flaws and trying to fix them. Thinking you have a defect that makes you ugly and deformed. Believing that others look at you to mock you. Always fixing and hiding a perceived flaw, hiding flaws with makeup/ clothes and comparing yourself with others. Avoiding socializing with others. You may see the flaws on a number of different body parts, however sufferers tend to concentrate on one part.

16 **Depression**; symptoms may include a change in sleeping patterns. Staying away from social engagements and appointments. Staying home alone. A change in appetite, eating too little or too much. Significant weight loss or weight gain. Becoming emotional for no apparent reason. A feeling of sadness, having highs and lows. Unable to make simple decisions.

17 **Drugs** (street drugs) with drug abuse, there are so many drugs on the market and the signs and symptoms very different. Therefore, I would advise you to look up on the particular drug to find signs and symptoms for it.

18 **Panic attacks**; symptoms may become very sudden, frightening and distressing to the sufferer. The feelings can be coupled with high levels of anxiety. The sufferer may experience heart palpitations, sweating, hot flushes and chills. They may have shortness of breath and chest pains. They may feel dizzy and faint, and this is just to name a few.

19 **Phobia**; symptoms, all phobias can cause depression and anxiety attacks. Sufferers often avoid the thing or place that cause them fear. An example is a person who fears spiders may not look or even want to touch a spider.

20 **Prolonged loneliness**; is a mental illness, and it can affect some people to the point where they may have symptoms that may include alcohol and drug abuse, depression, increased stress levels, suicidal thoughts, antisocial behaviour and the early onset of Alzheimer's disease.

21 **Seasonal affective disorders**; There are no real diagnostic test for this illness but symptoms may include feeling tired, depression, crying spells, poor sleep patterns and a loss of sexual drive.

22 **Self-esteem (low)**; when you have a low self- esteem, your thoughts about yourself is always negative; you may have feelings

that you do not deserve good things. You tend to focus on your weaknesses and mistakes and any problems you go through in life you will tend to blame yourself.

23 **Self-harm**; displays a wide range of behaviours and is usually a physical response to emotional pain. Some of the symptoms may include eating disorders, pinching, cutting and burning one. The sufferer may also abuse drugs or alcohol.

24 **Sleep problems**; prolonged: it is important to note that minimal sleep loss can take a toll on how you function during the day including a feeling of lack of energy, concentration, focus and your ability to handle stress. People who suffer from sleep problems tend to feel sleepy during the daytime. They tend to feel irritable and may possibly lead to other mental disorders.

25 **Stress**; is one of the most common mental health problem that we can all relate too. It affects us all in many different ways and can be daily. Learning how to manage stress and releasing it would be key to our survival in today's society. Some of the symptoms are a lack of concentration, getting frustrated, impatience, lashing out on others, shouting, crying, over eating, over sleeping, not eating sufficiently and a lack of sleep.

27 **Suicide/ suicidal thoughts**; symptoms may include talking about killing oneself. Saying things like I wish I were never born. Mood swings and or suicidal attempts. Saying goodbye to people as if they will not see them again and doing risky or self-destructive things like taking drugs.

Does this possibly mean we have all suffered from one type of mental illness to another at some point in our lifetime? Maybe. When it is not a mental illness that you are born with but have developed as a result of life experiences or choices, it can be very difficult to deal and cope with and very difficult for people to sometimes accept, largely due to the stigma associated with mental illness. People tend to not seek help earlier; families tend not to talk about it. Sufferers tend to struggle to cope on their own and mask the problem because of feelings of shame and failure.

My advice would be to seek help as soon as you feel that your life is out of balance, as soon as you feel and know your thoughts are not right or have changed in a negative way. Seek help as soon as the beautiful unison is in disarray in-order to regain the stability of body mind and spirit as quickly as possible, to get the help you need early on rather than later as when left it could be liken to leaving a wound to fester without treatment.

Chapter 4

Why some people are more affected by mental illness?

The gene factor and predisposition.

The new home

Whether I had the gene or not in this case was beside the point, I was heading down the wrong road regardless.

In 2013 when I moved into my new home, it was what I had dreamt about for a long time and I was really looking forward to the change and moving in. I got alllllll! Excited you know that deep happy feeling when you just want to scream and shout and say yes! I did it finally! I was already packed and ready to go. After a few months of moving in, the novelty worn off a little and I started to feel overwhelmed with everything, trying to get the house sorted and in order. I wanted to settle in quickly and was pushing myself way too much. I work full time and work was becoming **increasingly** difficult and challenging.

There were a lot of changes, challenges and pressures at work. I had just started an Internet based business, network marketing, which was taking up a lot of my time. Looking back now I was doing more of thinking about the business rather than doing the business it self. I was really throwing me out of my comfort zone but only in my mind. I was not happy with doing this at first because I like my own company and space and I had to attend meetings, speak to people, and be enthusiastic about network marketing. **Yes!** Be energized about it, but all I was feeling was low, simply because I was feeling overloaded and overwhelmed with everything that was going on around me. My husband was not well, I had concerns with my son at school, too much was going on. I felt that I was in the middle of my own personal space and everything around me was spinning at a very fast pace and I was just watching things happening but not really being able to take an active part in anything. So just imagine YOU! In the middle and life is literally spinning around you. Your kids, your spouse, hospital appointments, work, housework let's not forget that one, bills, throw in a little shopping, oh! And you have to remember everything for everyone, that's an important one, and going to the gym. This is really a minimal list because there is so much more that can be thrown in here but do you get the picture I'm trying to paint here. I felt I had lost the plot or better still did I even have the plot to begin with. Is there a plot? At this point going with the flow was not even an option, because everything was happening too fast and I could not keep up.

Don't get me wrong I wanted this network marketing business to work, as in time it would have enabled me more time to do things with my family and some financial freedom. I did put some time, energy and effort into the business but only short intervals, as it was all I could do at the time. I kept telling myself, slow down there is no rush but my mind and actions was going in completely opposite directions. My mind was out of sync with the rest of my body and there was no harmony, no balance. I was walking on a tight rope. I was on a slippery slope.

All sorts of feelings started to enter into my mind. Fear, doubt, sadness, joy, the sense of accomplishment, sometimes I felt enthusiastic sometimes I really didn't. I felt tired alllll! The time, I felt everything all at once. All the feelings you could conjure up, were there, and it felt as if they were there at the same time. It was a bloody roller coaster of a ride, which simply lasted way too long. Actually feeling overwhelmed was an understatement. Don't get me wrong, I was happy, but I felt overloaded with the move, work, problems at school with my child, my car was stolen weeks after moving and renting a car for some time became costly. It all seemed just a little too much, I felt like a failure. I had to relinquish my title of super woman and pack away my costume. I had to officially tell myself I no longer held the title. The pressure was on! The heat was on, and I had to show myself accountable, but to bloody WHO, and for what I thought to myself. There was no competition going on here so whom was I really tying to impress.

I felt alone even though I was in a house with four family members. I felt that something was wrong somehow and it is really hard to explain but I started to have feelings that I could not recognize and that was unfamiliar to me. We are not talking about a little bit of depression here I am talking of something much deeper from within, I had gained more weight after moving and was not happy with this either as nothing fitted. Everything seemed to be spiralling out of control including my weight and I felt helpless. I felt I could not do anything about it. I was in unfamiliar territory, another warzone, only of a different type. I felt I always had to put the best outside but inside I was crying out for help. I knew I needed to do something different, I knew that something had to change. I was feeling fed-up with everything; I was not coping at all. I had to count my blessings I was alive and fairly well physically but my mental health was strained extensively. I felt I needed to be teleported to another world where there was just peace and tranquillity. Where no one could bother me, speak to me, put demands and deadlines on me or ask me anything at all, so I could rest my mind and clear all the clutter in my head. But let's face it, that's not going to happen is it, I had to stop dreaming and get my head out of the clouds. So what was my contingency plan because you got to have one!

I knew I could not go through life like this, if I did I wouldn't last very long. Sometimes I felt like a headless chicken running around in all directions doing everything but not really doing anything properly. This has consequences it has repercussions to whatever the task may be. Someone once said you cannot chase two rabbits and catch any (4th Sept 2016)(Confucius or a *Romanian proverb) philosiblog.com;:http//en.wikiquote.org/ wiki/Romanian_proverbs#C.* Let's face it its multitasking gone really wrong. If a job or task needs doing, its worth doing right whatever that task may be.

Water off a duck's back

If we were to live our lives based on everything people thought or said about us, we wouldn't leave the house. We would all be sad and depressed beings. There has to come a point in your life when what others think or say about you has little or no effect. We must stand strong and be true to ourselves. We need to learn that in life there are always going to be people, who will comment on what we do, what we look like and simply how we live our lives, no matter what. Are we going to be angry with everyone? Are we going to isolate ourselves from the world or everyone we have ever known? No! We cannot live like that.

Words do matter, words are powerful and they do affect us. But let me unwrap this a little for you, we all need to be comfortable with ourselves, when you know who you are and what you want in life, and when you are heading in the right direction towards your dreams, goals and aspirations then what others say and think should not matter as much. Negative words should and can be like water off a ducks back. We have to allow ourselves to have a certain kind of attitude, one in which you must take positive criticism from others because that's how we learn, grow and develop, but at the same time allowing yourself to take your own path in life. All too often we are pushed and shoved down a route or path that only leads to regret, sadness and hostility, why? Because we just went with the flow. This is a saying I have repeated on many occasions; oh I will just go with the flow, but (*a quote by Andy Hunt*) *www.goodreads.com* (*4th Sept 2016*) said: only dead fish go with the flow. We are not dead beings, so I consciously try not to use that phrase and I think very carefully about the situation to determine if I want to go with the majority or not.

It does take a strong willed person to not allow negative words to affect them because it's certainly not easy and what others say and think about you do matter regardless. We are emotional beings and we hurt easily but as I said earlier we must stand strong be true to ourselves, when we are doing what we truly want to do, we are happy and when we are happy we are stronger and when we are stronger then negative words, comments or criticisms cannot knock us down so easily. We are then able to rise to the challenge of any situation and occasion without spot or wrinkle.

Our emotions run wide and deep, we have hang-ups about ourselves from childhood and we certainly don't need reminding of them as they are already etched into our brains like memory banks only showing their ugly heads when someone says something negative to us. Then all hell breaks loose because not only are we dealing with that negative comment but all the other stuff from the past as well.

The next time someone says something that is negative, think about their agenda because more often than not that person is not happy with themselves and when you are around negative, miserable unhappy people they want you to feel the same as they do. They make comments to you to make you feel bad about yourself and your situation, so they have the company they need. Doom and gloom, don't fall in the trap, stay away from the negative. Always remember unhappy people never like to see happy people.

Difficult situations

We all go through difficult situations in life but when you stay in that situation and do nothing or don't seek help and advice, because you believe you can handle it yourself, when you don't address it, that is when it becomes harmful and can mess with your mind. It is important to guard your precious mind and very important to safeguard yourself from physical harm in every way possible.

If you were in the middle of the road and saw a car coming at full speed would you not run as fast as you could for safety rather than standing in the road, do nothing and be harmed? This is the same for your mental health. Run like hell when you see the negative, because at some point you will see the damage it can do to your mental health if you do nothing. Your life could end up being unproductive and unprotected because you are exposed to harm and for too long then it becomes the norm. What is going on in your mind will and has to be manifested into your physical world; there is only so much you can temporally hide. People around you begin to see signs and symptoms that something is wrong. Yes, you will question yourself, you will also question your situation, but you need to seek help. There is a scripture in the Bible that says "Ask and it shall be given, to seek and you will find, knock and the door will be opened" (*Mathew chp 7v7*) Use whatever you can to fight for your life because we only have one life and we want to live it to the best of our ability and enjoy every moment GOD has given us on this earth. Fight I say fight. We are warriors of our own life and destiny, we have the power to change situations in our own lives, we have a certain amount of control so we should use it to our advantage, use it to better ourselves, use it to be as happy as we possibly can. The Bible talks about having a sound mind, which means having the ability to think clearly through adverse situations and being able to make decisions about your life that is right for you. Get your priorities in order. Another scripture talks about seeking first the kingdom of heaven and his righteousness then all other things will be added to you (*Mathew chp 6v33*) God understands your situation, He knows what is going on in your life but he needs you to recognize him also acknowledge him and him first.

So to wrap this up, having a predisposition to a mental health disease is one thing, basically it's really neither here nor there. Controlling your situations and experiences is what is important, how you cope and deal with them is what matters. You can control your destiny. You have more power than you think. Use it.

Chapter 5

Rate of black males in mental institutions

Pure illusions

The predestinations of the mystery of his will.
Quickened conversations have caused dispensations of confusions.
Hallucinations' no hesitations to be locked
away with our possessions.
Oppressions from our oppositions have not counted our opinions.
Accusations caused by obstructions, inhibits resolutions.
Impressions with no expressions has caused depressions.

Poem by Monika Minott

It is clearly evident that there are more black males and ethnic minority groups in mental institutions than any other race. There has to be an explanation for this and it is something that we should all be asking ourselves, talking about and trying to get to the bottom of. Whether it is through education, research, mentoring our black boys or right down to having our own schools. I don't think that segregation is necessarily a good thing but more action has to be taken to save our black men. Something needs to be done to reduce the high levels of black men going into institutions. Hearing about someone else's son or daughter, husband/partner or brother/sister becoming ill, should no longer be enough for us. It should no longer be acceptable for us, to go on our happy way saying well it's not my son or that person does not belong in my family so it does not affect me and it does not matter. It does matter! It does affect us all. It certainly has a direct bearing on the balance of the black families who tend to lack fathers, brothers, sons and at times black women who are then left to cope to run the household by themselves.

It would appear that there is a direct link between smoking cannabis and schizophrenia. It has been a culture for young black boys to join in the club by smoking cannabis for a long time now, it is well known. Could this explain why so many of our black men are in mental institutions, because of the long term affects of using the drug?

Research suggests that the part of the brain that is affected when a person smokes cannabis is the exact same part of the brain affected when a person suffers from schizophrenia. (*www.bmj.com*) 17th Sept 2016 if research suggests this, then why are we not doing more to advertise to black men against using the drug in this way? Why are we not highlighting it as a major issue to the state of the black families or something that has contributed to the state of black families in a negative way? Gang culture is also known to contribute to mental illness. Being in gangs puts pressure on young people to perform acts as part of an initiation process. This is sometimes traumatising to young people and I'm just touching the surface about the pressures of being in gangs and what effects it has on a young person.

Smoking cannabis and being in a gang, would play havoc on a young persons mind as to what they would be exposed too and the time they would be exposed to it.

I know a lot of work has gone into supporting our youngsters to leaving gangs by post gang members themselves speaking in youth clubs, schools, churches and so forth, but is this enough to make a change to the rates of people going into mental institutions? Is it sufficient to make that impact in a reduction of the high levels we see today. We are three to five time more likely to be admitted to hospital for more severe mental illnesses

It is imperative then that we educate young black men who smokes cannabis and anyone you know who may be in gangs as anyone can have and suffer from the negative effects of both. When the family unit has broken down and the father is absent from the home it can open the doors to young black boys to seek the father figure elsewhere. True to say this will not be the case for everyone and has not been the same for all black boys and men. Many black men and boys are very successful despite all adversity, but if you are told that your chances of developing a mental health condition was highly increased due to smoking cannabis, would your choices be the same or would you think twice. At least if people are informed about the long-term dangers, risks and effects of the drug, they can then make an informed choice. This will give all people a chance to make that all important decision on their lives rather than allowing our young people within our society to suffer peer pressure and end up on the wrong side of the road with a whole host of other problems to contend with. There are a lot of pressures on our young people today and they need not only our support from every direction but our wisdom that can be passed on through training, education, seminars and so forth.

A few questions to explore:

Are some people really prone or predisposed to mental illnesses or is this just a theory/myth? Is there really a gene that makes a person be at a dis-advantage? Or could it be that we are all vulnerable to developing mental health problems. Research have highlighted that there are more young black men and women in mental institutions than any other race. What is the root cause of this? Is it genetic as experts claim? Or could it be linked to social education and economic focus? Is there an element of racial discrimination?

This is a topic that I have been passionate about for many years as I have two boys and like any parent, I want the very best for them. But they have to grow into adults and I know I cannot protect them forever. So what do I have to do to ensure they are protected from this cruelty that life brings. How can I ensure that their lives will be full of laughter, joy and all that they want it to be? As a mother this is scary stuff. As with any other mother out there who just wants the best for her children.

When a particular race or ethnic group is predisposed to a particular type of disease they take measures. Measures to highlight the disease to the group, measures to ensure they minimize the risks that will cause the disease and this is done in a number of ways i.e giving information, encouraging people to gain knowledge about the disease, airing it in the news, holding seminars/discussions, tests, treatments ect. All sorts are done to create an awareness of the disease and how to prevent it or minimize the risks of getting it. What measure or measures are we taking or can we take for our black children, our men our women. What measures must I advise others to take to ensure their children do not go through this terrible illness? The numbers of mental illnesses have for many years been going up not down, so whatever we are currently implementing its sure not enough. We as a nation really need to address this issue more and put it on our entire priority list as first, before it becomes so large an issue we cannot cope with the effects and costs. Shame to say we will have on our hands a lost generation to mental illness.

One thing is for sure, is that the measures taken and the way we are treated as black people compared to our white people with a mental health condition is different and therefore the whole treatment and healing process is not always a positive one for us. As black people we seem to not only be in the system for longer periods of time but we get a raw deal in after care and alternative treatment. It would appear that medications are the main focus rather than using other measures and looking at holistic therapy for the recovery, healing and the treatment process. I don't feel all measures are taken into consideration when dealing with black people who are diagnosed with mental health problems. Not always having someone who really understands our fears, problems and issues, to make a difference is there. Meaning not enough ethnic minorities are in mental health professional positions to make necessary changes and a real difference to the society of black people across the country. But It's not only a black issue now it is an issue for us all, as many people white black and Asian are in the mental health system. And the numbers are rising. It is a time for us all to draw our minds together to make a difference to all not just one group of people but to all. It is now a worldwide issue, never have we been in an age where everything is at our finger tips and information is readily available to us all, but at the same time many are out there lonely and afraid to cry out for help or to speak out about what they are experiencing. Something is very wrong with this picture.

A beautiful experience

When I say that we need more professionals in the system that are able to relate to and understand our fears, issues and our life experiences, is because if I had told a doctor about the experience I'm going to tell you now, he would have probably first put me in a strait jacket, locked me up and throw away the key. This experience to me was a beautiful one, because I knew that what was happening to me and what I saw was a good thing, it had to be, because I was being released from something that night.

It had been about six to seven months in my new home after leaving a house that was haunted. I was still experiencing some problems of not sleeping well, having negative thoughts of being in an evil environment and that evil spirits were around me, but it was not nearly as bad as they had been before I moved. I was alone in my house feeling so happy and relieved that I had left the old house and as usual I would watch the God channel and take part in the reading of bible scriptures, praying and singing along with the praise and worship songs. This was the norm for me. On this particular Saturday evening I sat in the middle of my living room floor beside the heater, it was nice, warm and cosy, and as I said I was feeling happy and grateful for where I was at this point in my life and where I was coming from. There was a song playing that I really liked and I began to sing along. I lifted both my hands in the air, closed my eyes and began to worship, simply by thanking God. I was just being really and truly thankful to God for bringing me through my awful ordeal. My back was facing the door and as I began to praise and thank him I felt I wanted to continue to praise more and more, because I was so grateful for what he had doe for me. Within two to three minutes of worshiping, I started to see black cat like creatures running at full speed from off my body. They looked like cats and also rats but they were neither I could not really distinguish what they were. All I knew at this point is that I could not lower my hands and stop praising God. I was not scared, but I was shocked as to what I was seeing. I was not asleep or even in semi-sleep, I was wide-awake and fully conscious of what was happening and what I was seeing.

As I said earlier I had my back to the door, which was closed, and it would have not been humanly impossible to see my front doors. But I saw hundreds of black catlike creatures running at full speed off my whole body and running straight through the front doors. I held my hands in the air and kept worshipping until I saw no more. My physical eyes may have been shut at this point but my spiritual eyes were wide open to see the power and the glory of the almighty GOD at work and what he was delivering me from. I know without a shadow of a doubt that I was delivered from something or many things that night. I care not to know what. All I know is that God was at work and I allowed him to do what he needed to do by submitting to him through praise. I can honestly say that there is real power in praising GOD and I mean real spiritual praise not just lip service. I'm telling you this, to explain to you that no doctor or many doctors would have understood my experience or even be able to relate to it, and would simply think I was delusional, hallucinating and needed immediate help. Yes! I needed help all right but not help from a doctor, help from the almighty god himself. For many years I refused to even speak about this experience because of fear of what others would think of me, I'm glad I have the courage to speak of this experience now and release it from my life.

Chapter 6

Environmental factors

What are the external and environmental factors that can contribute to mental illness?

Could it be the lack of a healthy happy home, a happy environment and surroundings? Could it be spending too much time around negative, influential people? In my experience it is all the above and more.

Many factors can contribute to a mental illness, such as low-income families struggling to make ends meet and the pressures that puts on the family unit. It can affect not only the children in the home but the parents too, having to deal with worries on a daily basis of paying the bills and buying food, and just everyday living. All that goes into running a home can be very costly, the impact this has on how they live their lives is massive.

Some scientists have said in the past that there is no bearing on one's life with environmental factors to mental illness. Now I'm not looking at the molecular or genetic level of life and I am aware that it has been said that there is some who carry the gene that makes them predisposed to a mental illness. But I am going to argue this a little regarding outside influences to the mind and how much it can affect a person's mental health. Let me unwrap this for you, because stress can become chronic stress and you can experience stress in your life anywhere at any time for any reason and if left untreated, meaning left without resolving the issues, problems, or concerns can then manifest into long term depression, isn't this a mental health condition? The cause an environmental factor? Yes it is. Being able to surround yourself with the right people in an environment that works for you can influence the outcome of how you behave, think and feel.

I don't know much about schizophrenia and have not done studies on the disease but I have witnessed a close family member who I will refer to as P who was diagnosed with schizophrenia some years ago, my experience and observation is that certain environmental factors contributed to help the disease manifest. These were times when p had her own flat, she did not see family members often, at times she missed her medication and there were little interaction with friends or acquaintances.

I noticed that when the environment was changed coupled with other factors; such as being in the company of positive people, a different country, and interacting with friends and family the manifestation of the symptoms of the disease was reduced, off course with medication. The change did not only create stability in normal behaviour for that period of time Ps environment was changed but a sense of happiness, having hopes, dreams and goals returned. There had been times when P started looking at her physical health and looked at ways she could undertake physical exercise to reduce her weight and live a healthier lifestyle. P took action towards these goals and looked at other ways to improve her appearance, which showed me motivation and positive thinking. I would not think this is the case with just one person. So whether it was being in another country, being around positive people, going to church or interacting with more people, I know It did make a difference to the life of P and I saw it time and time again.

When P came back to the old environment of being in the flat alone the symptoms slowly started to manifest itself again and was more prominent. P became depressed again and paranoia kicked in, despite taking medication. The doom and gloom came back over a period of time and the need to return to the better environment was pursued over and over again.

This shows that some environmental factors play a large role in the manifestation of symptoms of mental illness. We can assume this would be different for everyone, because individual experiences are diverse and medications may work differently from person to person.

It could be difficult and costly to prove and sustain by professionals and individuals but one person not being in the mental health system is not only worth it but would and could save a persons life from being shattered by a mental illness.

Other environmental factors such as

Poor housing

Loss of jobs and being unsure of the future has put massive pressure on individuals.

Suicidal thoughts, In which some people have committed the act itself. In 2014 alone there was over 6,581 suicides in England and Ireland. These are alarming figures and one we should not ignore.

War and the effects or aftermath of war, plays a large part in how people behave because of what they have seen and experienced, and the effects on people not only losing their homes but a whole way of life and living. Seeing loved ones die in front of you has major traumatic affects, long lasting effects not only on adults but children alike, who has their whole life ahead of them with the memories of living through war.

The fact that you have no means by which to feed your children, having to watch them suffer starvation and possible death has to be one of the most traumatising experience parents have to endure.

A very stressful job, having to meet deadlines on a daily basis, targets, the overload of paperwork, the pressures you bring home because you are still stressed from a day's work, and how that affects the family unit? These are just a few factors that I have highlighted to you; there are many other external factors that can contribute to mental ill health.

This is a little story of someone I know well but will refer to as Mick, who was experiencing problems that if left would have probably ended up in the mental health system along with medication and long term stay in hospital. It does not take a lot to get you to this point but it can be hard to get out of the system.

Have you ever felt down about your life, whether it is work, family or friends? Have you been stressed about your own personal problems? Well I can tell you that I have, to the point where I stopped all day-to-day activities. There was a point in my life where I was so stressed about my life and about my then girlfriend, about work, studies to the point that I stopped going out even to university. I had to reduce my working ours to 2 days a week. My then girlfriend was my first love and I will always have a place in my heart for her. I spoke less to her as the time went on and every day for about three and a half months I kept to myself not speaking to anyone as much as reasonably possible and if I had to speak I would fake the smile. A reserved perfect smile to trick any person, I needed too. I had a problem, I didn't know what it was at the time but I also didn't need anyone in my business either. I planned to fix it myself, to fix my own problem. Now looking back, I feel like I'm only just understanding what my problem was. I was not happy at all. Being happy and feeling happy is very important and can impact on your life greatly. Now let me explain, at the beginning I was happy but slowly over time I realized that something was making me unhappy. Something that was part of the core of my life, Looking back now I can see clearly it was my university life. University was something that at the time I thought was a good step forward as anyone would.

I wasn't very fond of school or even college. Personally I think the education system is wrong. I feel it does not help young people achieve anything. It assembles large groups of different individuals under the same system, under the same umbrella in the hope that everyone will come out ok. After weeding out those individuals that don't fit into its standards. I don't have anything against education or schools; on the contrary I think it's a great thing to be educated and to go to school. But I feel there is a great lack of life experiences that should be captured during your early years of life, during time in school, colleges and universities. I now realize that university is not for everyone and it was certainly not for me. Only now that I have begun to realize and understand that by engaging in something you enjoy, things that fill your heart and spirit with joy, that satisfies the soul, is real happiness in my opinion. I also feel that finding true happiness in life is one of life's goals. It gives a truly satisfying feeling and a real buzz for life. As I mentioned before, I had a problem and I did not enjoy going to university, it's not that I was unable to do the work; it was just the fact that I simply did not enjoy going and being part of that world anymore. Even though it was a subject that I handpicked myself and was really interested in doing. One of the main reasons I went to university was because of my mother who really wanted me to complete my studies, as well as the all the good intentions of all my aunts and uncles at the time. I felt pressured to attend university and make the most out of my life. In all honesty I did not have anything else to do other than me looking for a full time job. I was eighteen at the time and as you know looking for full time employment with no experience and qualifications and starting on the adventure called real life was a very daunting prospect to me and I was not prepared for that. It was a road I was not prepared for or ready to venture down. So, I thought I would take the easy route and delay that road called real life road for a few more years and delay the process of work, house and the responsibilities of bills.

Mick's story highlights some of the external pressures that can play havoc ones life, on anyone's life. Mick lives in a happy home, where food and warmth is provided, bills are paid, clothes on his back. In this case there was no physical need but rather an emotional one. Giving up a university course was a drop in the ocean compared to ending up in a mental institution. Keeping sane was more important than anything in the world because without sanity you have no stable happy secure life. Nothing and no one is worth taking your healthy mind away from you. It has to be guarded using any means necessary. A healthy mind is a healthy life. Mick has given up his university course and is working full time. But the main story here is that he is happy, he no longer feel pressured into doing something he doesn't want to do and if in the future he decides to go back to university, then he would ensure he is ready to give it 100% and that it would be his decision only.

Chapter 7

Coping

How we cope with the stress, challenges and emotional baggage of life is what matters most. Some people cope much better under pressure not because they are stronger but because of their coping Strategies and mechanisms. How they perceive situations, their support networks that steps into play when most needed. Something they tap into, sometimes almost automatically. It could be something they do, somewhere they go, someone they speak to that supports them to cope in a better way. Are some people simply smarter in how they deal with situations and experiences? I'm not saying that people who don't cope well are not smart, but they simply think differently or react differently. *An English proverb (15195) (www.worldofproverbs.com)* says a problem shared is a problem halved. It's so true, why carry the burden alone? Sometimes just sharing a problem with someone can automatically release you from that problem or situation, you feel better. Sometimes you even come up with solutions to the problem yourself.

If you were at the airport and had six large suitcases would you struggle to carry them all by yourself? Or seek help whatever that help may look like. Imagine some people are carrying baggage's from childhood, what a very heavy load to carry? You realize you were not the favourite child, a teacher said you will never amount to nothing, a friend said you're a user, your employer has told you that you're not a good worker and your job is on the line. Whatever it may be, emotional baggage especially from childhood can be very challenging to cope with, to say the least. Emotional baggage is very heavy loads to carry around on a daily basis. These loads weigh you down in many ways and they do affect the way you interact with others or the way you work and generally live your life from day to day.

Emotional baggage can cause people to be on the brink of a breakdown, or literally throw themselves off the edge. Emotional baggage and the stresses and strains of life can be as weighty as physical luggage. And what!! Never putting that baggage down or releasing it in any way, shape or form and having to perform at work, be a mother, a father, a sister a brother how on earth can you possibly be any of these things effectively, efficiently, lovingly or even be happy really happy doing any of these jobs if you have so much baggage, so much weight to carry. But we do it and we do it all the time, we keep sweeping things under the carpet and carrying on as if nothing is wrong.

We must make every effort and take every step to ensure we look after our mental health, just as we would take care of our physical health. The fact that we cannot physically doesn't mean we should ignore it, the effects of what you are feeding it or not feeding it will manifest sooner or later into your life. Taking care of you is first taking care of your mind because everything first happens in the mind then it is manifested physically into your life. A healthy mind, spirit and body is what we all should be striving for, finding the balance that is necessary to be creative and productive, having a life that is able to flourish in everything we do with no hold backs or barriers. This is what was intended for us all by the almighty God. Striving always to achieve in a variety of ways, making an impact on each other positively and affecting lives as we embark on life's journey.

We should all instil in our lives, subjection, discipline and order not only to keep us on the right track but to enable us all to achieve what we were destined to do and be. Yes, It's a fight most definitely, yes! It's hard, but without the fight we cannot develop, change and grow. So embraced the fight, the difficulties and march on to your higher calling. Invest in yourself; invest in your mind just as you would invest in your physical world. Find the gifts that are within you, work it and deliver it to the world. We all have something that we are naturally good at and that is your gift. Your gift maybe unique to you but whatever it is or are, single or multiple use them to make your mark on the world use it to your advantage.

You (going out)

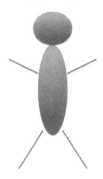

Family children work friends bills house work appointments partners

You cannot serve on an empty vessel. There has to be a balancing act in your life in order for things to work and for your life to run as smoothly as you can possibly make it.

All these will take from you, every time in every way possible, they are all demanding. You will find yourself in a real mess if nothing goes back into **_YOU_** to keep you safe, secure and generally free from too much worry and stress. It's sad to say that the list above can be very selfish at times and will always demand your attention, **_your undivided attention_**. It is therefore imperative for you to realize that time for **you** is just as or even more important than everything else that is going on in your life. When bills are due they don't wait, children always want your undivided attention, work is becoming more and more stressful, demanding and challenging. The list can be endless. Don't forget this list is daily.

> If you had a thousand pounds in your bank account and you kept taking money out but putting nothing back into the account, it would only be a matter of time you would end up in the red and in trouble.

You (going in)

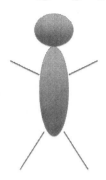

hobbies   relaxation   rest   doctor   exercise   healthy   eating

(and more)

All these processes and many more are very important to **_YOU_**, it is imperative that you keep all appointments, doctors, and dentist, eye appointments ect. Watch your health, because no one else will. Ensure you exercise on a regular basis. It is a well-known fact that exercise reduces stress levels, and while stress itself may not be an illness, too much stress over a long period of time can cause illnesses.

Rest, when you can, put your feet up and don't feel guilty about it. Take up a hobby; and do something that you enjoy. Read good healthy positive material that will make you feel good about yourself and give you inner strength to deal with life and whatever it brings. Feed your body with good wholesome food.

These diagrams are just simple equations on how to create and maintain a balanced lifestyle. There will be times when physical illnesses cannot be helped but when approached with a positive attitude and positive thinking it can help to ease the pain and trauma of what is going on in your life, in-order to live well and healthy we must first do for ourselves. Stay away as much as reasonably possible from negative people or those who make you unhappy about yourselves. Feed your minds with good positive material.

Another important factor to recognize is that without giving back to yourself this balance in your life will feel out of sync to you. You will be extremely tired and feel that way all the time. Your diet will end up being of poor quality. You will feel irrational, ratty and even aggressive at times. Your thinking and focus will be unclear and your patience and tolerance will run to zero. Everything will seem too much to handle. Ultimately you will end up losing because your physical health will start to deteriorate. **I'm no doctor** but I have had my own experience, I can now assure you I'm no super human. I'm not saying that everything will be fine but I can give you comfort in knowing that you will be better equipped to deal with life, to handle challenges and to fight back.

Don't take it lightly

Don't take what I'm saying lightly, if life is a series of events, tests, experiences and gifts. How we react to them daily matters greatly. Your reactions to all of these activities form your life and how you live and we all want to have a good life. We are presented with baggage we don't want, not ready for, situations we cannot cope with, and we wouldn't even give a second glance too, or didn't ask for, they are handed to us anyway, this is life. Some gifts you give away, some you put down and never use, some we use straight away. Some we don't recognise and therefore never utilize. Unexpected situations can be a shock to your whole being because it was presented at a time you felt vulnerable, weak and unstable.

Life has a way of throwing a number of situations at you at a time when you're feeling confused, bewildered, ashamed, sad and depressed, or just when you thought things could not get any worse. When I say situations I mean anything, **ANYTHING** that life gives. What I'm really trying to say here is you must be ready for anything life drops at your doorstep. The good and the bad

Chapter 8

Types of help available to you.

There are so many ways to find help within today's society and so many different kinds of help available it can be endless.

The Internet
Counselling services
Medications
Mentor's
Self-help books/videos/audios
Family /support groups/therapies
Friends
Group sessions, support and help from schools/colleges/ universities
Religious help (such as temples, mosques and churches)
Charities (Sane, Mind, Together, Breakthrough, Depression alliance and many more
Brochures/leaflets- (giving information, direction sign posting)
Online chats and courses (be mindful online)
Rehabilitation
Substance abuse programs
Yoga
Alternative medicine
Music therapy

Even though most of us struggle to live and maintain a healthy lifestyle, there are groups that we can join to help us along the way for:

Living a healthy lifestyle
Exercising daily
Eating healthy
Having a healthy social life (Interacting with others)
Having goals and aims in your life
Positive thinking
Having routines
Hobbies/activities

Allow yourself the time and effort in the above list; as these do take time. For one to promote healthy living and a healthy lifestyle, when your state of mind is in total disarray it can be very difficult and will need will power and motivation on your part. Give yourself a break; don't put too much pressure on self. Take baby steps and when you feel strong enough then move to your next goal and then the next, then the next. It is most important for you to take some responsibility for yourself and your own life. There are other groups, resources and services within the community that you can tap into for help and advice. The list above can be endless.

I understand that it can be just as easy to shut yourself off and away from the world when you are in the wrong mind-set. It's the last thing you would want to do when you feel unwell is to go and speak too, seek help or see someone about it. This is understandable but you have to push yourself to get the initial help.

As I said before, If you have a broken limb, would you sit in your bedroom without doing anything about it? Would you not go to the hospital or the doctor to get it seen to straight away? Ok let's go to a toothache shall we. Now really! Would you sit in your house with a bad toothache and do nothing? I'm sure you wouldn't? Why! Because the pain would be so unbearable you would not be able to bear it. I know I have said the same thing over and over and in many different ways but it is just to reiterate the importance of the point I'm trying to make each time and if I can say the same thing in a million different ways so you get it loud and clear I will. If I can get someone to recognize signs of their mental health condition early enough to make a difference to their life and the outcome of it, even one person then it would be worth it. It only takes a click of a button on the Internet to get the info and help you need and in seconds you can make a start on what organization you want to use.

There are so many self-help books on the market today that will help you in your everyday life. You can pick choose and refuse. You can specify exactly which self-help book you want and make a start on really living your life to the full. Many audios and videos are also available for self-help. Listening daily to them and applying the principles to your life can promote motivation and positive thinking, which can lead to and can promote the beginning of healing, when there is emotional hurt. There maybe someone you know who goes to church and you could ask for his or her advice. It could be a friend, a neighbour, a colleague or a family member. A lot of religious institutions now have support systems in place for people who are struggling and need help. Religious help does not always mean you have to go to a church; many counselling services are religiously based. If you're not happy with asking any of these people, there is always counselling services that are available which are confidential and are not religion based if that's the kind of support you need and want. Not everyone wants to go to a religious based organization. They could also refer you to other services that are available to you. There are leaflets in doctor's surgeries, community Centre's, libraries, churches ect. Don't be afraid to take one.

There are many medications now on the market that is able to suit your need depending on what you are going through but **seeking advice from your GP is of uttermost importance and should be first on your list of priorities and actions to take**. A doctor will find what is suited to you and your situation. I'm not saying you have to be on medication for the rest of your life but your GP will always advise you on your course of action.

If one to one does not work for you there is always support groups/workshops where you can talk to others who are going through the same or similar experiences as you. There are mentors in schools/colleges and universities across the country all you have to do is ask, don't suffer alone, don't be afraid to ask.

Substance abuse of any kind is not easy to break; will power alone is sometimes not going to cut it. At the tap of a button on your computer you can get help almost immediately. Look at joining groups that can help you and offer the support while you are off the drug.

So there you go, the world is truly your oyster, make of it what you will, but we only have one life make the most of it. There is a saying that I always use to say and it's this. God did not promise tomorrow to anyone, we don't know when we are going to leave this earth and by what means. So while we are here let's make the most of it. God did give us this earth for us to live happy and enjoy it, so let's really start living.

Chapter 9

My experience

My two and a half year hunted experience

In 1999 I moved into a little 2/bed house not far from the flat I previously lived in for six years. I was happy for most of the years I lived at that flat, but not only was it too small for my son and I, but he was now about six years old and needed his own room.

A young man moved into the flat above me who had mental health problems. For that final year in the flat I went through hell with the noise he would make at night. Talk about noise pollution. I definitely have experience in that. He would constantly shout and bang all through the night, the only way I could explain it, is it was as if he had a large fully loaded barrel, which he slammed to the ground constantly while shouting. I know this was not possible but that's what it sounded like. I don't know what he was using to make that noise, looking back now it could have been a piece of heavy furniture but it was scary most of the time because I thought at any minute now the roof was going to cave in and kill my son and I.

I was so fed up with the constant noise night after night that there were times I would go up and knock on his door to tell him to shut the f...K up, but little did I know I was putting myself at great risk of being hurt by this man. He was clearly psychotic and delusional because of his actions and what he was saying. I believe now at times he was also very scared himself as to what he was experiencing. When I would knock on his door he would open it and shout Run! Run! Run! They are coming after me. There were times when I certainly wasn't going to ask him who was coming after him and why, I would just say my piece then dart down the stairs. The house was usually in total darkness, pitch black, I would tell him to shut up, stop the banging, and that I could not sleep then run down the stairs as fast as I could in fear. It took some bravery on my part at times, but when faced with noise pollution to that extent and level you have to take matters in your own hands. Sometimes when I was going up the stairs I was usually scared and trembling, I felt the fear but did it anyway just to get some peace.

There were times when talking to him did work, he would be quiet for a little while which gave me a mini break. But it would start again after about an hour or so. This went on during the last year I lived at the flat. I used to wonder why no one came to visit this poor man. There was no family and no professionals, none that I saw anyway. I wondered if he was taking his medication or if he had any to take. I wondered if he was eating because he was extremely underweight. I remember times I would see him walking around the village and he would acknowledge me and say hello. I would feebly nod reluctantly with anger that I did not have sufficient sleep the night before because of the noise he made. Thinking to myself another black male who is mad.

My breaking point. It was the summer holidays and mom came over from Jamaica to see us all. I had invited her for dinner. I cooked a lovely meal then went to pick up my mom so we could spend a little quality time together catching up on things, people and events from Jamaica.

When I came back home with my mom and son we locked the car door, my son took the keys for the flat and opened the front door. He ran into the flat and almost immediately ran back out saying mom! Mom! There is water in the kitchen. I ran into the flat only to find water! Dirty water streaming down my kitchen walls. My kitchen did not have any windows so when you were in it, you would need to turn the lights on. If my son had turned the lights on he could have been electrocuted. I'm so glad he didn't turn them on. At this point, this was my key to getting in-touch with the housing for the millionth time to ask for a move. Eventually sooner rather than later a property became available and I went to look at the house with my sister and the housing officer. I accepted the house with no hesitations. Soon after the paper work was completed, I moved in to a more suited accommodation. Well so I thought at the time. I so wanted to move from the flat, that I totally ignored my sister's prompts to not accept the house. I was happy to be moving, well, for five minutes at least.

The day I moved in, my mother decided to stay overnight so she could help with unpacking and settling us in. The first night I slept like a baby, totally dead to the world. You know what it's like! Moving can be really exhausting stuff. So we got up the next morning and I was feeling relieved that I was in the house and with a smile on my face I turned to my mom to say good morning. She asked almost immediately, did you not hear me shouting you to turn the on lights last night? I looked at her in shock horror, No! I replied why? What was the matter? I asked, She told me that there was a man coming up the stairs with two little boys complaining and saying this is there place and why was I here. I shook my head in confusion, bewildered. She further described the man to me and said she had to go to the top of the staircase to send them away. She explained that she didn't actually physically get up out of the bed but it was like an out of body experience but seemed real to her. I could see that she was shaken up and very disturbed by the ordeal, she was shaken by her experience and she certainly didn't seem happy at all. I could also see the tiredness in her face and almost a hint of worry. We had a little discussion then went downstairs to make breakfast. I thought to myself she just had a bad dream or something.

Mom stayed over for a following night as there was much to do and she wanted to help. At this point I definitely wanted her to stay, as I was a little disturbed by her experience the night before. All was well for the day and we had forgotten what happened the night before. We just got on with the unpacking, busy busy busy as little bees.

My second night, I was still very tired, so I naturally fall asleep. We woke up the second morning and mom explained to me that she had a very similar experience to the one the night before. She had told me that this time the man had put the two little boys in the cupboard downstairs and tried coming up the stairs himself. Mom said he was very angry this time. She wrestled to send him away again, obviously with no help from me, as I was fast asleep. She told him that he should not be here and that he needed to leave. She did not rest until he had left. This got me thinking now, about who this person was from the other side? Why was he coming here? How long was this property empty for? Many questions fled through my mind and I became a little intrigued. I also felt I had jumped out of the frying pan and straight into the fire. I am now suitably housed, so what could I possibly say to the housing association to get out of this one. Fear came over me as I thought to myself, I'm stuck; I'm going to have to live through this one.

As time went on I began having experiences of my own, but different ones. I could not see anything but I could sense that I was in an evil surrounding. There were many nights I would have nightmares. One night I dreamt that my son was standing in the corner of the room and I could not see his face as he had both hands covering his face. He was crying profusely. I sat up in the bed and questioned him saying what are you doing in the corner? And moreover why are you crying? I then remembered that my son stayed over at my sisters for the night. It didn't take me long to realize that this little boy, standing in the corner took on the form of my son and this made me very angry. I leapt towards him to grab this evil imposter when suddenly he vanished into thin air. This was the only night and time I felt I had actually seen a ghost and it was scary, really scary, because the experience was real to me. Another night when I was unable to sleep although very tired, I called my sister and asked her to come over for company as I had work the next day and needed to sleep. She slept in my son's room and my son slept with me. Well! When she got up the next morning she was quite beside herself asking if I did not hear her calling and shouting my name all night. She said something evil was in the room and she did not get a wink of sleep. She was a little reluctant to talk about it and she didn't come back to stay overnight after that night. It seemed that if anyone else other than my son slept over they would have the agony of the nightmare and evil presence and not me but those nights were few when I had someone stay over. Many nights I myself was unable to sleep, the only way I could explain my lack of sleep is it felt like every time I was about to fall asleep I was going to fall off a cliff. Then in-order to stop myself from falling I would end up jumping out of my sleep. Other times I felt I was being stifled and could not breath and struggled to wake up. Having this nearly every night was just horrible.

I started to ask the neighbours about who was living in the property before me, what had happened to them and how long they lived in the property. There were many questions I needed answers too. There were a couple of Caribbean families living in the property before me. The family I was told about first, by my neighbours did not fit the description my mother gave me but they lived in the property for some time, maybe over ten years, so my options were limited now as I could only speak to the neighbours who lived in the avenue for more than ten years. The other family who lived in the property before them was also there for about ten years. That narrowed it down to two sets of neighbours. Only one of my neighbours was willing to talk and acknowledged what my experiences could have meant. Not that the other couple was not nice and pleasant, they were, just not approachable in that way.

So this one neighbour was a very nice man, very friendly, approachable, one who was willing to spill the beans a little and give me an insight into who **THE OTHERS** were. Meaning the other family that lived in the house before the last ones are you following me. My neighbour lived in the avenue for over 15 years and remembered the first family well. Well it was confirmed that it was another Afro Caribbean family with two little boys, not sure of the ages possibly around six and eight. The mother apparently was mentally ill and in a mental institution which left the dad to care for the boys. It was suggested that the boys were possibly being mistreated or abused. It was said that the boys were locked in the cupboard downstairs and the father was experiencing troubles himself, as the pressure was too much for him. It appeared as if the father was not coping.

He described how the man looked, his height, complexion and that he always wore a cap. Now this description fitted the one my mom had seen strangely enough down to the T. My mother never saw a woman because the woman was never there; she was in a mental institution, well back then. Basically I'm telling you I had moved into a haunted house. These people were obviously dead or some of them were, I didn't know what to think. Actually I would rather not have to think too much of this past experience. But still the story had to be told.

What the hell was I going to do now, as I was in what the housing would call a suited accommodation? Frankly I was stuck.

I carried on as normal but trust me things was far from normal I could not sleep at night. I knew that the lack of sleep would eventually send me over the edge. Each night my sleep would be disturbed and interrupted because I felt something evil was in the room with me or due to a nightmare. I could not see anything, I could not hear anything, nothing was moving around the room, I could only sense I was not alone and I'm not talking about my son either. An unknown strong evil presence was always there at a certain time of the evening nothing would happen in the day we were like a normal little family during the day but at around 9 pm things would change, the atmosphere was different, there seemed to be a shift in temperature and an airy scary ambiance and if anyone knows me I'm no weather girl but I can sense a chill from afar and It was chilling, and I was scared.

By this time my mother returned to Jamaica and I was alone in this little haunted house. I tried to make things as normal as possible to minimize the disruptions to my son. I decorated the house keeping things as positive as I could. I ensured he was as happy as he could possibly be at the time but it was not easy even to do that. Thank God he was a happy little child anyway and one who was not easily perturbed by what was going on around him.

Months later another one of my sisters came round to visit with her granddaughter, she decided to stay over for the night, we had a lovely evening, chatted, cooked, ate, watched T.V then we all went to bed. Again she had a very similar experience. Only this time when she woke in the morning she told me that she fought all night in her sleep. She said she had seen a little girl who wanted to take the place of her grand daughter; this little girl was angry and questioned my sister asking why was she there? And she was not supposed to be there, and that she must leave. My sister said she was tired as she felt she was in a battle all night. As news about the house spread within the family, I had less visits, basically they all stayed away so I felt alone and lost even more.

I started to ask more questions about the family who was in the house just before me and found that they also experienced problems but it would seem of another kind. There were many issues with a number of their children and some had been taken into care, the ones that were left at the home were very problematic at school and I guess at home. I went back to the housing to try my luck of getting another move, but it was not happening. They were not going to move me and that was that. I thought I was going mad at one point, as I had just moved and there was no evidence of anything happening, the property looked just fine, well to look at. But I knew something was not right, I could feel it, I could sense it, but who could I turn too at this point, who would understand what I was going through and who was going to help me out of this one? I did go back to the housing association on many occasions to argue my point but I would always get funny looks as if I was now the mad woman saying strange things. There were times I was extremely tired and looked rough and I would decide to go to the housing in anger and frustration, so I could imagine what they must have thought of me. Unfortunately for me they were not taking this one on board. If wasn't not a problem they could see and fix then it was not in their category.

There was one time when my sister came over again but this time during the day. After doing my normal chores I decided to do a little washing and hang some clothes on the line, as it was a nice day. So my sister and I went out, we hung the clothes on the line and while we were coming back inside the house we noticed things in the garden. It was not you're normal looking rubbish but odd bits and pieces, strange things. Odd looking dolls almost voodoo like stuff. I say voodoo because when we looked at the bits and pieces that's what came to both our minds at the same time. Little beads and old little candles. It just did not feel right or look right. In hindsight we should not have even touched the items but we were naïve and we just did not think.

So I sought a priest, a pastor, clairvoyants, Jehovah's witnesses, whom I studied with for a while and basically anyone who claimed they could help me, anyone who would listen, and anyone I could drag off the streets. It cost me money I never had but it was worth it, as I needed to sleep, I needed to rest my mind and body. I was going off my head with the lack of sleep and worry of what would become of my son and me. For some reason I still managed to function. I took my son to school every morning then went off to work, did the best I could on the job. I picked up my son from the child minders went back home, cooked dinner, and ate then it would all start again.

This went on for two and a half years. There were times when we would be fine and I thought to myself this is it! The OTHERS have gone. Whatever it was is gone but it had not gone I realized that I learnt how to block it out of my life, a strategy I used to survive. I started to sleep early in the evenings while my son would be up watching TV so I was getting some sleep just not a good night's sleep like everyone else. That's how I managed to cope; I slept for a good couple of hours from around 6.30 to about 9.30. Luckily for me I had an angel for a son, he was so good he would allow me to rest, poor thing when I look back at him and how much he must have missed out for that two-and-a-half-year period saddens me. But I think he was secretly happy that he had full control of the TV for a number of hours before going to bed. He was happy that he could watch all his favourite T.V programs without disturbances from me. Luckily for me my son was not affected with this evil. It only seemed to affect me. Don't ask me why or how but he was able to get on with his life unharmed by this experience. I thank god for protecting him.

There was a time I could not see my carpet; it was covered in newspapers. Every evening I would buy newspapers to look for a suitable property that was affordable for my son and I. But could never find anything that was affordable and that was near my son's school. In addition to that I really wanted the housing to move me but they did not recognize my problem as being a problem, as far as they were concerned I was already adequately housed. They were not going to move me, so I was left in my own mess, So to speak.

At this point Family members had refused to come to the house and most of the times I was left to deal with the problems myself. I decided to stick it out even though times got very difficult I would pack up all my stuff hoping that I would find something, and for months live like that, then I would unpack saying to myself this thing is not going to beat me. But I was fighting a losing battle because I could not fight with the unseen or the unknown, my problem was a spiritual one, an evil one which was not that easy to overcome and fight and it was not going away no matter what I did. I met with a number of people throughout the two and a half years, spirit mediums, pastors; I spoke and studied with Jehovah's witnesses. All did help my **state of mind** even though the situation stayed the same.

This is what my message is to you. Even though your situation may not change straight away it is imperative that you guard your mind in the process using anything and everything that is positive and I say positive because some of the people I spoke to or used to help me with my experience and situation was not what I would call positive now. If you don't guard your mind you could lose yourself in the situation and be lost forever. This is life; life has a way of throwing all sorts at you and you have to find the necessary help and support you need to get through it.

Only one sister was a constant support to me during my time at the haunted house, but I had other people around me that I could talk too and who offered help in ways that took the pressure off. My sister would encourage me and always gave advice. She would even stay until late evenings when things got really bad. There were times when I had to call her in the middle of the night 2-3 o'clock for me to go over to her house just to get some sleep before work.

God's got my back

Well one evening I was informed by my sister that my brother was going to move house, he had bought a property. This was great news and I was happy for him. He was living in a 3/bed house and was going to move in a matter of months. A thought from my sister became a reality the only sister who stuck by me in my ordeal said well why don't you just move into his property as he is leaving. At this point in my life I was really depressed and I was not excited about any idea as I felt I had tried everything already and nothing worked. I shrugged my shoulders as I thought my life is just going down the pan what makes you think he is going to agree, what makes you think this is going to work. We had a short discussion about it I made the necessary phone calls he agreed to me moving into his old property and before I knew it I was packed and ready to leave my haunted experience. Hip hip hurray.

Happy times

I lived in my new property for thirteen years as happy as I could possibly have been. Thank God I took the opportunity and followed the idea and advice of my sister. If not, I would not be writing this book right now; I too would have ended up in a mental institution and possibly with my son in care.

Sometimes life hands us things, things we wish not to have but these things whatever they may be only come to make us stronger a more resilient people if we don't allow our problems and situations to break us. I did spend a lot of time during my ordeal watching the God channel, reading the bible and spending time with positive people who were able to uplift and encourage me to stay strong. This is very important in order for you to stay afloat of your situations whatever they may be. Talk about it because it helps to release the fear and the stress of it all.

Chapter 10

Recognition

Whatever your belief is, as to where or when the problem started or came from is sometimes beside the point. The point is that you recognize that you have a problem and that you seek help and medical advice immediately.

Don't ever blame yourself for having a mental health condition; unfortunately it is sometimes circumstances why you are in this problem. Rather look at how you can minimize the effects of the illness you have, think of ways to improve self. I know this cannot be easy because when you are not well it would be the last thing you are thinking about but you would have times when you are well enough to think about it. We can spend too much time on the what's, the who's and the whys but at the stage when you realize that help is needed, then seek it. Eventually as time passes you could go deeper into psychotherapy and other treatments to see how things got to the stage they did and how to possibly prevent it from happening again. I know that some people will regress but do try to keep up on your medications and other treatments that will give you the stability you need to stay strong and keep working on you.

It didn't take me long to recognize that all was not well with me and that I had to do something about it. To start moving into another direction as I knew that if I didn't I would have been in *deep deep* trouble and it would have been really difficult for me to pull myself out of the trap and web of depression even with help. What was wrong? Well a whole host of things, I was doing too much, not getting the well-deserved rest I needed, my car was stolen, pressures at work, there was countless challenges from every end. Let's face it, too much was happening in a short space of time. Talk about too hot to handle this was too much to handle. I needed time, more time to deal with what was going on in my life at the time.

I suffered in silence because I never spoke about any of my ordeals until now. There were many times I would write. I found that it was helpful for me, sometimes I would just write down my feelings, which came out in the form of poetry, but it was an outlet for me that I used which was great at the time as it was an immediate fix. I felt I had offloaded my fears on paper then literally put it to one side. It felt good to me. Somehow I felt some release as if I had spoken to someone.

You can have outlets, many outlets, to off load your cares of the world but when your mind is closed to them you don't see them, you tend to not use them. They are in fact **CLOSED DOORS** to you at that time; they are no good to you. One of the most important things to do when you have feelings that are not good, positive or uplifting is to release them by any means necessary. Speaking to someone, a friend, a family member anyone that you feel you can trust and that you feel comfortable to express yourself too. Try doing something that is uplifting whatever that may be. Something that makes you feel good about yourself, something that releases those endorphins, anything that will make you feel proud about yourself. What I found worked for me was listening to music. Music that was soothing and calming, but also something I could have a little giggle too and immediately bring up my mood. Music that can and would take me away from the pressures of this world and placing me in a zone of my own or something that was so relaxing that it allowed me to reflect on my hopes and dreams but also the events of the day and putting things into perspective. Releasing the bad energy is important for you as built up anger and frustration can cause harm to your wellbeing.

This year 2015 I'm going to make it alllllllll! About me. I am going to take care of my spiritual, mental, physical and emotional wellbeing as much as reasonable possible and with all the strength and willpower I can conjure up within me. I am going to answer back when I need too, defend myself when I can and remove myself from negative people. Be around like-minded people like myself who have aspirations, hopes and dreams and who have a positive outlook on life no matter what is going on around them. I have let myself go a little. Missing important appointments, not taking time out for me, not resting when I needed too. Don't get me wrong I will do what I have to do for others, but I will be a little selfish and put more me myself and I in the picture the time.

You cannot serve on an empty vessel and I can relate to that, I think I was serving and running on empty for a while. Simply look at a car! If the car has no petrol it cannot run so why do we think or feel we can live a happy, fit and healthy life when you do not feed the mind and body correctly with good wholesome healthy food and material. It's only a matter of time that what's going in your body will manifest outwardly. One thing I have learnt over the years is how important it is to take time out for you, to do whatever it is that you enjoy whether it's watching a movie, going off to an exercise class, baking, reading, sewing there is a plethora of interesting things we could all be doing. Do anything that can be therapeutic, relaxing and enjoyable to you. Yes, YOU.

Most definitely easier said than done but this is one of the most important things you must do for **SELF**. You, very busy moms out there who are juggling 50 plus balls but catching none, because the baby is crying, you're on the phone to the housing officer because you're in rent arrears, you have put on loads of weight but your still going to the gym even though you are not eating right. Well! I know because you have to pick up the kids from school and they are likely to be hungry so you prepare quick and easy processed food under the oven why? Yes, I know it's quick and easy and not much thought has to go in that. I understand because I have been there, done that and most definitely worn the t-shirt. I'm here to tell you, don't beat yourselves up you are doing your best and if your best is not good enough well so be it. Do what you can until you can do better. You are all heroes, Heroes I say. Your main aim right now is to take care of you however that may look to others.

Staying sane is about forgiving yourself on a daily basis to what you have done wrong and those who have done you wrong. It is about asking God to forgive you. Throw the pain away because it will hinder you from progressing in your life and the life of your children.

The life diagram

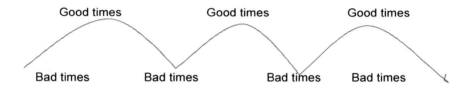

This is life, things happen and they happen all the time good and bad. Whoever said life would ever be easy and smooth sailing with only good times. No one. So why when the bad times comes along, we cannot seem handle it. Why aren't we prepared for the bad times? It's the bad times that shows us who we really are, it's the bad times that shows us what we are made of, our stamina how strong we are and how resilient we are. As I said earlier in the book embrace the bad times, In some situations, it's what drives us to be better people and it's what drives us to want more out of life. The thing is life will not always look like this, at times life may seems like the diagram below, only few good times and many periods of hard times.

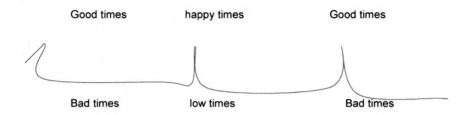

Good times   happy times   Good times

Bad times   low times   Bad times

There are times in life when the bad times, seems forever, long lasting and back to back, one thing after the other. At times there will be no let up on the bad times and only short bursts and intervals of good and happy times. Long-term stress will ultimately cause chronic stress, which can lead to depression.

Stress can set the stage for more serious mental health conditions. This is the time when creativity steps in, when you have to pull out all the stops, draw on all the resources you can. Think of different ways to cope and to manage. Think outside the box because at times when it rains it pours. You will need that all-important backup system that is within you to step into place to survive.

When all the lights in your house go out, because of a blown light bulb, there is a backup system, a switch to switch all the lights back on. There is a backup safety system that is put in place to regain your lighting system. This is the same with your body and mind; you must find your backup system within you. Find your inner switch. You will need it, when life becomes difficult.

Chapter 11

Effects on family

The effects on family, friends and the general public are sometimes very daunting, scary and unpredictable. It is a very traumatic and challenging time and experience for family members to see their loved ones go through a mental health crisis. It leaves them feeling helpless and inadequate as there is usually very little they can do to help the situation, especially when a loved one is going through the diagnostic stage. As a matter of fact, any stage of a mental health crisis can be daunting, traumatic and very sad. When you're loved one is well and taking their medication, there is always going to be that thought in the back of your mind of hope that they stay well.

The life of your loved one at crisis point is left in the hands of professional strangers such as psychologists, psychiatrists, doctors sometimes police officers (police officers are not involved in diagnosis), therapists, counselling services, social workers and more depending on the diagnosis and the severity of their condition. That leaves little room for you the parent or carer apart from worry and hope.

As a family member you may have to sit and listen to professionals telling you what medications is best for your loved one, what hospital they will be admitted too, what treatment plan is laid out for them, again depending on the diagnosis, how long the treatment is going to last for and the severity of their condition. If you are a parent your loved one will always be your little boy or girl no matter what age they are but when your children become ill, it tends to heighten feelings of worry and fear for the carer for longer.

It is a difficult time for the family to see intervention by all these mental health professionals and having to just go with the flow because we believe they do know best and work in the best interest of our loved ones.

Don't get me wrong all these mental health professionals are very important to a person who has a mental illness. These are the people who are going to and have to shape, control and contain the situation or situations.

They are the ones who will be looking at issues and managing them the best way they can, afforded the resources and knowledge they have about the person in question is sufficient

But a family member can be left with feelings of loneliness, inadequacy, loss and failure from their experience and situation. At times, they may feel ashamed and they themselves will feel and become socially isolated and question why me or why us? and may feel robbed.

What support is available out there for these people? Who have loved ones experiencing mental health problems? It is understandable and sometimes reasonable when a loved one tries to contain and manage the issues at home alone. They detach themselves from what is really happening and will sometimes decline to talk about their experiences or challenges, as if it were not happening or that they have not noticed the changes. They may also see it as a shame to the family and a failure on their part, However, cultural norms, customs and beliefs can determine the way a problem is viewed and addressed.

It can be a lonely road, and at times, one you sometimes have to walk and do alone, but I want you to know that you are never alone. There are many support groups out there that can help you through this difficult time.

Suppose you decided to take a long trip on the train, you buy your ticket, wait for the correct train to arrive. When on the train you find yourself a seat and maybe even buy something to eat. The train begins to move, there you go! enjoying the ride and the view. The grass is green; you see a few animals grazing in the field. The sun is shining; it's a lovely day. There is a little smile on your face. You feel at ease and comfortable.

The lights start to flicker on and off then Suddenly it becomes dark, all lights are off now and you cannot see or hear a thing. All is quiet and you realize you are now in the tunnel. You have to go through the tunnel to get to your destination. You wait patiently, you don't like it because it makes you unsure, a little nervous maybe, but you have to sit tight and wait until you have reached the end of the tunnel. You cannot leave the train; you cannot say to the conductor that you want to get off the train, because you are nowhere near where you want to go and where you want to be. You cannot ask for your money back, as the ticket is non-refundable. So you have to sit on that train and wait for it to go through that dark tunnel. Sometimes life seems like a dark long tunnel ride but there is always light at the end of the tunnel. We just need to sit tight, wait and be patient as hard as it may be.

In life we go on many journeys, some good some bad. Some long some short, it's a journey non-the less. Sometimes it's a journey we have to go alone, at times we have company. If you find that you are alone on your path it won't be for long sometimes it's a journey only you can take, it's very hard its heart-breaking but never give up and stay strong. It is easy for me to say stay strong but I have seen a loved one go through a mental health crisis and I have had the feelings of helplessness and sadness myself. As I have said before stick with it, it does get a little easier; get the support you need to get you through the difficult times.

Chapter 12

Statistics to mental health

If in todays society where doctors, counsellors and therapists are so readily available, then what have we been doing? What has gone so terribly wrong for us? How could this be? Living in a so-called modern society that we have so many people, men, women and children in mental institutions and in the mental health system. Computers and phones are in homes across the nation and information is more readily available than ever before and at the touch of a button so what could we possibly be doing wrong for the stakes to be stacked up so high against us? Is it a lack of understanding, recognition, realization or lifestyles? These are questions I know many of you might be asking yourselves.

Our mental health system is in overdrive and it's strained so much that some people who are ill and need support, slip by without even being noticed. On the other hand the number of people seeking help has been steadily rising over the years and continues to creep up on us.

Prevention is better than cure, but I think it's a bit late in the day for that thought. I hate to be a pessimist and a bearer of bad news but we need to deal with the backlog of people already in the system, these people need to be introduced back into a society with full help and support and one (society) that will not reject them but welcome them with open arms. I know this is not the case with everyone experiencing a mental health condition, some do get the right support they require from friends, family and professionals but at the same time many sufferers find it hard to integrate back into society because of the stigma to mental health.

It's important that we try to prevent others from entering the mental health system so where do we start? I say from the beginning. As we have talked about earlier in the book, there is a whole host of factors causing mental illnesses, such as broken homes, war, gangs, drugs, poverty, predisposition and physical illnesses and more. Seeing that none of us is immune to any of the above list then I say working on our state of mind is the most promising factor there is and one that we need to hold on to. Having the right attitude and being in the right frame of mind despite all adversity is what we all need to be striving for. If we don't we will surely continue to head down the road of world mental health destruction. If we start at the beginning and work our way through together we will see some changes and progress.

When I say the beginning, I mean from childhood. If you were given a precious gift, one that is absolutely beautiful and one that you had always wanted you would take every precaution to safeguard that gift. You would keep it in a safe place and protect it, maybe even take out insurance for loss or theft. When we are blessed with children, they are precious gifts from GOD.

It is our **DUTY** as parents to guard them mentally, physically and emotionally during their early years of life, because these are the most important of a person's life. These early years are when we are most vulnerable to abuse and trauma which can manifest through mental health problems in adulthood). What our children is exposed too and the lifestyle we provide, makes a massive impact on them later in life.

We must do our uttermost best to seek help and advice as soon as we feel something is wrong with our children so they can get the best possible intervention early enough. It is our duty to ask questions, and question the responses we receive from professionals and make sure we are receiving the right support for our children. They (Our children) are the next generation.

You could say, well! I'm an adult it's too late for me. No it's never too late to start living your life to the fullest, it's your God given right. As I said no one is immune to what can cause a mental illness, but how we handle our problems is what is going to make or break you. The key to the stability of good mental health is dealing with the issues in your life head on and in a positive way rather than negative. When looking at an athlete running the hurdles, each time that person reaches the hurdle they jump. Unless that person is injured physiacally, they jump. It is a natural instinct; it's the nature of the race. Life is full of hurdles, setbacks and disappointments but you have to face every hurdle like you would in a race and continue to run grabbing your help modes along the way

I would like to say to all mothers, fathers, brothers and sisters you know your loved ones best don't wait for crisis point, seek help and advice contact your doctors, councillors, your churches whoever you know will help your loved ones before its too late, before the crisis point. Our approach to people with a mental illness that has blighted thousands of lives each year has to change. We must tread carefully and with caution but also with urgency. We need to realize that it is a problem we must all take on bored not wait and sit back but one that needs all our immediate and direct attention.

Chapter 13

Stereotyping

A statement I read during my research into mental illness and I thought was very powerful.

Some said they had no friends or had lost friends when they were diagnosed with schizophrenia, including one man who said his friends "disappeared like leaves off an autumn tree after he was diagnosed as being mentally ill." www.healthtalk.org

How sad was this statement, when you need a friend most in your darkest hour of need, friends leave you. I'm not saying that these people who walk away are bad people, they simply do not understand and are fearful of what is happening to you. People find it hard to talk about mental illnesses and tend to avoid you. Sometimes because they don't know what to say to you. Also, over the years we have heard so many horror stories in the media about people who are mentally ill, we just assume that everyone is going to be of the same severity and this is simply not true.

Believe me I have had my fair share of negative experiences of people with mental illnesses and some I would rather not talk about. Some turned out to be quite funny, none the less it was scary. I remember when I was still living in Jamaica, I had left secondary school and I wanted to go on to a nursing school. My parents were not able to send me due to lack of finances so I completed a year of practical nursery nursing instead. A position became available and I was slotted in.

I lived with my cousin in Kingston and was able to do this I year course with ease. We had uniforms like real nurses and I felt this was the nearest I was going to get to nursing school for now so I embraced it. I was able to do something at least as my options were limited. There were six girls on the course and we all became very good friends; I was just loving it. About half way through the year we realized that we were being targeted. Most evenings when we came out of the nursery to go home, a mentally ill man would try attacking us by hurling verbal abuse and running after us. I don't know if it was the uniforms, the color of our uniforms, how we looked or just that we reminded him of someone in the nursing profession? but he would lay wait us outside the nursery and as soon as we started walking to the bus stop he would start to run after us.

At times we were ready for him and started running straight away after coming out the nursery, other times we saw he was not there and half way down the road we would see him coming after us sometimes with a big stick in his hand. Because it was six of us and we were always together we had fun with it but I tell you I was scared as hell at times. This carried on for a while. Sometimes when we were running we used jump over peoples stalls as the bus stop was a distance away and people were on the road selling foods and goods. I think this is why it was so funny at the time. No one ever reached out to help us but on the odd occasion women who sold on stalls would shout out to him saying leave the girls alone! This is always an experience when remembered I would have a little chuckle over, as no harm came to us apart from panting and gasping for breath when we got to the bus stop and finally jumped on a bus. This was also a time when we would split up and disperse so I guess to him it was not the same. He always targeted us when we were together.

The stigma of mental illnesses is diminishing slowly, because not everyone is locked away from society in mental institutions but rather is integrated within our communities. But we still have a long way to go. This is not just an issue in this country but it is a worldwide issue and a major concern, so how we think about and support a person with a mental health condition has to change.

I pray this book will help in breaking not only the stigma of people in distress from a mental illness but the silence of the people suffering and crying out for help. I hope that people who feel they are vulnerable are able to recognize signs early and seek advice and help. It is alarming the amount of people in this county alone who suffers from a mental health condition and end up taking their own lives and who was afraid to speak out because of fear and stigma. **Be silent no more.**

Physical vs Mental: My thoughts

People tend to be more concerned with physical illnesses rather than mental illnesses. They think and seem to relate to it in a more positive way. So if I broke my leg or had the flu or cancer even I would get more support with that than having a mental health condition. I would receive get-well cards or flowers and visitors. I would have time off work to recover and many other types of support would be given. People cannot and still refuse to show compassion when the illness is a mental health one and this is still a taboo subject for people to talk about and one that they will shy away from.

We will sympathize with someone if they said they were little depressed and feeling low, even though this can be and is also a mental health condition if left untreated and left to get worse. Society would be able to relate to it better because it is very common compared to if I had a diagnosis of schizophrenia. This is the breaking point the breaking news for society when you actually get a diagnosis saying you suffer from this or that, and depending on the diagnosis this is when people will start migrating from your world and before you know it you are all alone with an illness you don't know how to deal with.

There is a real stigma with mental illnesses, which needs to be addressed and I mean addressed properly. Not only by the government by pumping more money in the mental health system and into schools but churches need to play a bigger role a leading role. When people are being shunned not only by society but also by their own families then I feel religious groups should step in, to play the role of surrogate family for people with mental health conditions. There is so much more we can all do to help make the lives of each other especially those with a mental health condition better and easier.

Here is a series of seven short positive poems that will get you in the mood to kick start you for achieving a goal, that will get you shooting to the stars of stability, happiness, peace and love in your life. I wish you all the best in your life's journey.

1) Power

Compete with thine self, for there is none higher
than you and him who is within you.
The inner workings of the mind strive
always to be the best of the best.
Show it, work it, breathe it, live it.
It's you, go to the core from when you began, dig
to the deepest, and clime to the highest.
Seek, look, knock, ask your way to the truth
of you. It is you that binds, that
finds, that has the power over minds. It's you.

2) Goal

Compete with thine self, you have arrived.
Optimism is the key; the dream is your goal.
Let it ponder on your mind night and day, till
you smell it, taste it, vision it and feel it.
Reward yourself already its yours, it's there, take it, own it.

You have arrived it's me and mine, mine and me its self.
It is all you have; it is all you need.
The goal is the key.

3) fear

Compete with thine self, beat your own score.
Rise high to the occasion feel no fear, come
forth from wenst thou cometh
stand alone, stand strong, stand tall and shine.
Jump the hurdles, the obstacle, face all judgements.
Fear has left, feel no fear.

4) Motivation

Compete with thine self, drive your way to the top.
Just do it, why wait, why hesitate. Don't
stop begin now; it's now or never.
Shock yourself into action, move toward your peak.
Enhance your skills, the higher is calling you.
Motivate from within, sync with your calling.
Motivation is fuel.

5) Stability

Compete and stabilize yourself humming bird style.
Hover with the stars, that's where you
belong. You're a bright shining
planet with much to offer. Find your zenith from deep within.

Stability is crucial to your inner light, the
inner universe that lies within.

6) Challenge

Soar like an eagle, glide through the skies.
You are at the height of yourself.
Powered by the wind, you cut through the clouds.
Energise you! Be you, there is none other.
You are unique. Challenge the un-challenged.
Triumph over the challenge.
Victory is yours.

7) Complete

You are at peace with yourself and well grounded.
Tranquillity is inside, wisdom has taken root.
You are at one with the almighty.
You are now powered; you have achieved your goal.
You have no fear, you are motivated.
You have stabilized yourself and challenged all.
You are now Complete.

Closing statement

The reason I wrote this book is because up on till this point there has been many times I thought I was going to lose my mind. Life has a way of throwing you from pillar to post and trust me if you are not strong and if you do not work on yourself daily and constantly; you most definitely can lose it. There really is a thin line between sanity and insanity.

I want to help you to truly believe that god has put you on this earth in this time to live your dreams and to inspire others. It is partly our responsibility to take care of our minds because our minds control and hold our hopes, dreams, aspirations and visions. So it is vital to discipline, love and care for our minds as we would our physical bodies it is our greatest asset in life.

by Monika Minott

Bibliography for book

www.healthline.com

www.mayoclinic.org (dissociative disorder)

www.nhs.uk (anxiety disorders, personality disorders, obsessive compulsive personality disorder, post-traumatic stress disorder)

www.dbsalliance.org (mood disorders)

www.psychguides.com (psychotic disorders)

www.mayoclinic.org (eating disorders)

www.wikipedia.org /wiki/impulse. (Control disorder)

Psychiatrycentre.co.uk (the London psychiatry centre) (bipolar disorder)

Healingabout.com (about religion)

Verywell.com (depression)

nhs.uk/conditions/panic-disorder/pages/symptoms.aspx (panic attacks and phobia)

www.m.webmd.com (pre-disposed of the gene to mental health)

time-to-change.org.uk (charities)

community counselling services, INC. American Psychiatric Association. (1994)

Diagnostic and statistical manual of mental disorders, fourth edition. Washington, DC: America Psychiatric Association.

En.wikapedia.org/wiki/acute-stress-reaction. Article talk (stress response syndrome)

www.medicinenet.com/seasonal-affective-disorder-sad/article.
htm (seasonal affective disorder) (causes of mental health)
mind.org.uk (low self -esteem) for better mental health
selfharm.org.uk (self-harm)
Helpguide.org (sleep problems)
Mental health foundation www.mentalhealth.org.uk/stats statistics
to mental health in the UK then worldwide categories.
Mental health association (symptoms to mental health)
http://www.healthtalk.org/peoples-experiences/mental-health/
mental-health-ethnic-minority-experiences/discrimination-
mental-health#ixzz3xK8oJ4pT
https://www.mentalhealth.org.uk

Acknowledgements

I would first like to thank my husband Glen, for supporting me. The support he gave, allowed me the time to write this book, which was very important to me. A Thank-you to both my son's Remel and Zeekiel who both not only had an input in the book but encouraged and prompted me along the way. Almost like cheerleaders. Giving me the guts, stamina and the strength I needed when things got difficult. A special thank-you to Rachel Craven my Manager, who one day handed me a book and said she thought of me. From that day I started to read more and the more I read the more I believed in myself. The more I realized I wanted to write. This was the spark I needed to begin this book. A thank-you to another manager Tom Mullan who was always a support to me along the way in ways he would never thought himself. At times a tower of strength to me and always gave the right advice and encouragement. Sharon Nembhard a work colleague who always told me that there was a book inside me and for years I carried that thought around with me and now it has materialized, so many thanks Sharon for seeing the potential in me what I had not seen in myself for years. Other cheerleaders were Marcia McKenzie, Vivia Thompson, and Verona Smith my sisters who played a big role in helping me with this book. Marcia always said to me to put my poems in a book. Hear it is Marcia, it has been more than a book of poems, and it has been much more than you bargained for. I managed to put a couple of my poems in. vivia who helped with finalizing the book and Verona who was my rock of support in the earlier years of bad experiences.

All these people and more had a big hand in my life leading up to this point and I want to say thank-you again for all your support, expressed thoughts, love and acts of kindness. It has helped me to be the person I am today.

About the Author

My name is Monika Minott and I am married with 2 boys. I currently work as a day centre officer for people with learning disabilities; I have worked there for many years. For most of my life I have worked in the caring profession and I love and enjoy what I do.

I immigrated to Jamaica in 1981 with my parents then returned in 1988.

Throughout my life I have faced many challenges and experiences, which led me to right this book. I have always felt sadness and a passion towards people with a mental illness, and I have had close encounters with them over the years.

Writing has always been a passion of mine but mostly poetry; I love the play on words with no rules.

I thought it about time I wrote this book, as it has been on my mind to do for many years and would like to support others who may be struggling to cope in life.

Lightning Source UK Ltd.
Milton Keynes UK
UKOW02f1511041216
289102UK00001B/60/P